Noah's Ark
and the
Ararat Adventure

John D. Morris

You may already know the story about Noah and the Ark. You may know how Noah took pairs of every kind of animal into the Ark so that they would be safe during a time of terrible destruction. You may even know that the Ark landed on the mountains of Ararat, where Noah's family and the animals left the Ark to start a new life in a world so dramatically changed.

But there is much more to learn from this story. Why did God send such a Flood? What was the world like before the Flood? How could water cover the mountains all over the earth? How did Noah get all of the animals into the Ark? What happened to the animals and the people outside the Ark? And what happened to the Ark after Noah left it? Does it still exist today?

Today, many people are searching for Noah's Ark, and others are trying to increase our understanding of the world that was destroyed during this great Flood. What an exciting subject! I hope that you enjoy sharing some of the adventures and mystery surrounding Noah's Ark and the Flood.

John D. Morris, PhD
Institute for Creation Research
10945 Woodside Avenue North
Santee, California 92071

January, 1994

Master
Books

Foreword

In recent years, we have begun to explore the moon, the solar system, and the universe around us. Many new discoveries are being made every day with the help of powerful telescopes that enable us to see far into space, and plans are being made now to further explore the stars.

But even though we are continually learning more about outer space and our solar system, there is still much we don't know about the earth and its past. Was the earth once covered by water? Did Noah really build the Ark and take the animals on board to escape the Flood? And if so, what does it mean to us today?

To find answers to questions like these, I have become involved in one of the most exciting adventures possible: the search for Noah's Ark!

Walking on the moon made me more aware of the beauty of the earth and its God-given, created ability to support life, while walking on Mt. Ararat made me more aware of God's protection of His people in this world and His judgment of sin, not only for the people of Noah's day, but the people of our day as well.

I have been involved in the search for the Ark since 1982, while Dr. John Morris has been involved since 1971. John's background in geology prepared him to understand the effects of the Flood on the earth and Mt. Ararat, and he knows nearly all there is to know about the search for Noah's Ark. His personal experiences on Mt. Ararat, including being struck by lightning, are truly thrilling.

In this book John presents a Biblical view of the Flood and the earth's past, as well as its wonderful future, in addition to describing the search for the Ark. Most importantly, he has explained the message of Noah's Ark in a much-needed true story that will benefit everyone who reads it.

Noah's Ark and the Ararat Adventure is one of the most accurate, entertaining, and educational books available for would-be explorers of all ages. Readers will enjoy it again and again.

Col. Jim Irwin
1930 – 1991
Ararat Explorer and
NASA Astronaut

Noah's Ark and the Ararat Adventure

First printing: 1988
Sixth printing: June 1999

Copyright © 1988, 1994 by Master Books. All rights reserved. No part of this book may be used or reproduced in any manner whatsoever without written permission of the publisher, except in the case of brief quotations in articles and reviews. For information write: Master Books, P.O. Box 727, Green Forest, AR 72638.

ISBN: 0-89051-166-7
Library of Congress Number: 93-80508

Library of Congress Cataloging in Publication Data
    Morris, John D., 1946 -
    Noah's Ark and the Ararat Adventure
    1. History — Juvenile literature
    2. Noah's flood

Printed in China

Table of Contents

Chapter 1

The Lost World

Imagine that you could visit the world as it was before the Great Flood of Noah's time. Imagine that the sun is just peeking over the horizon. It is morning in the forest. The animals are starting to move out of their dens, nests, and burrows where they have been sleeping. Their movements are joined by those of the night animals returning to their homes.

The search for food is not hard for these animals. The forest is rich with many kinds of plants that can be used for food, and there are plenty of smaller animals to be hunted. In the forest, trees, shrubs, and many colored flowers are abundant. Plants and animals in this forest are great in number and variety. This forest is very different from the forests that you can visit today.

As the morning mist rises from the ground, songs of birds join the other forest sounds. But if you listen closely, you will also hear strange sound that you have never heard before. Over in a sandy clearing by a stream you can hear the peaceful clucking of a mother duck-billed dinosaur as she takes care of her newly hatched babies. Suddenly, you are startled by a deep roar from within a dense jungle of giant ferns and thick vines. It's the call of a huge tiger, a giant cat with long curved teeth. The roar reminds you that this is also a world full of violence.

Leaving the forest, you move toward the grassy plains. There are tents in the distance. As you approach you can hear the sound of sheep and cattle. In the camp, men and women are beginning their morning work. Some of the older children are shouting while they chase away a family of small chicken-size dinosaurs from a garden near one of the tents. Nearby, a young man checks the thorn barrier protecting the newborn lambs and calves huddled close to their mothers. These people are related to a man named Jabal (Genesis 4:20). It is even possible that this is his camp.

Far off in the distance is a great city. Outside the city you see many small farms in which grow all kinds of plants that are good for food. Although people work in the fields, most of them want to spend the night within the safety of the city. Behind the city wall there are many houses—and each house looks like it is built to protect the family within from its neighbors. This city was built by a man named Cain, and is named after his first son (Genesis 3:17).

From somewhere in the city comes music played on a flute and a harp. The musicians were taught by Jubal, who was the inventor of these musical instruments (Genesis 4:21). It must be a party, but from the sound of the arguing it doesn't sound like much fun. From another part of the city comes a different sound, the clang of hammers beating hot iron and bronze into weapons and tools. This place belongs to Tubal-cain, whose father brags, "I have killed a man for wounding me and a young man for hurting me!" (Genesis 4:22-23).

The violence and the wickedness of this world have not gone unnoticed by God. The Creator is sorry that He has made man on the earth, and His heart is broken by the evil that He sees. Soon God will destroy this world, and every person and every land animal will be destroyed as well. But one man—Noah—and his family, have obeyed God, and they will be saved (Genesis 6-8).

How can We Know What the World was Like Before the Flood?

How do we know anything about the past—the time before we were living? We can learn from people who recorded what the past was like. Sometimes they leave records that truthfully tell what the past was like, but sometimes they don't. The story of the Flood is like that. The Bible records the true account of what happened; but there are also many legends told by people who changed the real Flood story to fit their own purposes. Today many

truthful records of people who were actually there. Fossils are one such kind of evidence. Have you ever seen layers of rocks with fossils of plants and animals inside? You probably have. Billions and billions of fossils have been found all over the world. There are billions and billions of fossils that have not yet been found, and there are billions and billions of fossils that will never be found! What caused all of these fossils?

In most cases, fossils are the bodies of animals and plants that died when they were suddenly buried in mud. The mud later dried and became hard rock, keeping the shape—or even actual parts—of the plant or animal saved in stone. But what caused all the mud? The best answer is Noah's Flood, and when we see fossils, we should remember the Flood and why God sent it.

If we refuse to believe the details that God has provided in His Bible, then it becomes much harder to understand the past from the evidence that we see around us. It is like trying to know what a jigsaw puzzle looks like with only a small number of pieces. God has told us what the

Trying to understand the past from a few fossils that are dug up is like trying to put a puzzle together without knowing what picture is on the puzzle and without having all the pieces. You might never get it right! But with the true history of the world given to us in the Bible, we CAN understand the fossils and the past. Most fossils were laid down by the horrible Flood recorded in Genesis.

people don't know why the Flood happened and most are told that it didn't even happen at all.

There is other evidence of what happened in the past, although it is usually not as clear as the

world was like before the Flood, and now the pieces of evidence that we find finally begin to fit together.

The World In the Beginning

In the beginning, the world was different from the world that was destroyed by the Flood. The Bible says that Adam and Eve, the first two people God made, walked with God in the Garden of Eden. From its description in the book of Genesis, we know that no place as beautiful as this exists on earth today (Genesis 2).

The animals lived in peace with man and with one another. Adam and Eve did not kill animals for meat. They ate from the plants and fruits of the Garden, as did all of the animals that were created then. Adam and Eve were made so that they would never die. Every day there was sunshine and a mist would come up from the ground at night and water the many plants in the Garden. It was a time of health and happiness (Genesis 2:5-6).

Adam and Eve also had plenty of work to do. They were responsible for caring for the Garden and the animals that shared Eden with them. But God had given Adam and Eve a warning. He told them not to eat the fruit from a certain tree—the one that He called the "Tree of Knowledge of Good and Evil." God told them that if they ate fruit from this tree, they would begin to die! (Genesis 2:15–17).

There were many other delicious fruits, nuts, and vegetables in the Garden which they could eat. But God wanted to see if they would be obedient. You see, God had given Adam and Eve everything that they needed to have a perfect life so they would never die. Now it was up to our first parents, Adam and Eve, to obey their Creator or to rebel against Him. It would be their choice.

Adam and Eve Choose

Genesis tells us that there was another creature in the Garden. This creature, named Satan, hated God, not because of anything that his Creator had done to him, but because of his sinful pride he wanted to be like God and rule in God's place (Isaiah 14:13–14).

One day Satan, secretly using the body of a snake, came to Eve near the forbidden tree. He told lies and changed the meaning of what God had said. Satan said that the tree would make her just as wise as God. He told her that she would not die, and that God didn't want her to eat the fruit of the tree because He did not want her to be equal to Him (Genesis 3:1-5).

Eve saw that the tree's fruit looked pleasing. She thought that it would be good to eat, and she wanted to be just as wise as God. Eve decided to disobey God and ate the fruit. Once she had eaten the fruit, she took some to Adam. Satan did not need to deceive Adam into disobeying. Even though God had been so good to them, Adam chose to rebel against the one rule that God had given them. (I Timothy 2:14)

But, of course, the fruit did not make them wise like God. In fact, it made them realize how foolish and small they really were. They knew that they had disobeyed, and then, to make things worse, they tried to hide their disobedience from God. They knew that God hates sin and would have to judge and punish their sin of disobedience. And He had promised that the punishment would be death (Genesis 3:6-13)!

The Promise

But even though God had to punish their sin, He loved Adam and Eve. He wanted them to ask for forgiveness and to be friends with Him again. So he told them of a marvelous plan. He promised that one day a woman would have a Son who would take their punishment for them. That woman would be a descendent of Eve. When that Son grew to be a man, even though He would be wounded by Satan, still He would

conquer Satan, ending the evil and death caused by sin. Since the penalty for sin is death, this special Son would come and die for the sins of the whole world, and become the savior of the World. This Savior, promised by God to Eve and Adam so long ago, is Jesus Christ, God's Son, who died on the cross as a punishment for their sin (and our sin, also) (Genesis 3:15), and then rose from the dead, giving us victory over sin, death, and Satan, too (I Corinthians 15:55–57).

Because Adam and Eve were responsible for caring for the creation, their sin also brought death into the world (Romans 5:12; I Corinthians 15:21). They were driven out of the beautiful Garden. Until Eden was later destroyed by the Flood, an angel was sent to guard the Garden and keep anyone from returning to it.

The Effects of Sin

Outside of the Garden, Adam and Eve found that the world had changed. They had to work very hard to grow and gather their food. Some plants began to grow thorns and others could not be eaten. No longer were Adam and Eve able to live peacefully with all of the animals, for the animals had changed, too. Worst of all, every living thing began to die. Through violence, sickness, or old age, each person and each animal would die (Genesis 3:14–24).

All of these things reminded Adam and Eve how horrible sin really is. And each time they would see a meat-eating animal make its kill, touch a plant with thorns, have to work hard, or see someone die, they would remember that the God who loved them and who had given them only good things, also had to punish them for their disobedience.

As time went on, Adam and Eve had sons and daughters and their children had more sons and daughters. At the first, of course, brothers and sisters had to marry each other, but this was not a problem until much later, when the effects of sin on our bodies were much greater (Genesis 5:4).

Sooner or later everything died, but most things lived a long time and many things grew to large sizes. Adam lived for almost a thousand years after his creation (Genesis 5:5). In fact, it was not until after the Flood that God allowed the life of humans to last only about 70 years or so (Psalms 90:10). But until the Flood, all of Adam and Eve's children, grandchildren, great-grandchildren, great-great-grandchildren, and so on, also lived long lives. Even though sin had changed the world, it was still a more pleasant place to live, compared with the world today. There were still no storms and many animals were peaceful.

But each day people became more disobedient. Before long, people everywhere laughed at the idea of obeying God. By their violent and wicked lives, they showed that they hated God. There were still some people who loved God, but they were few. The people who still loved God tried to get the others to come back to God, but the people would not listen and continued in their evil ways (Genesis 4:26; 5:22 and Jude 14–15).

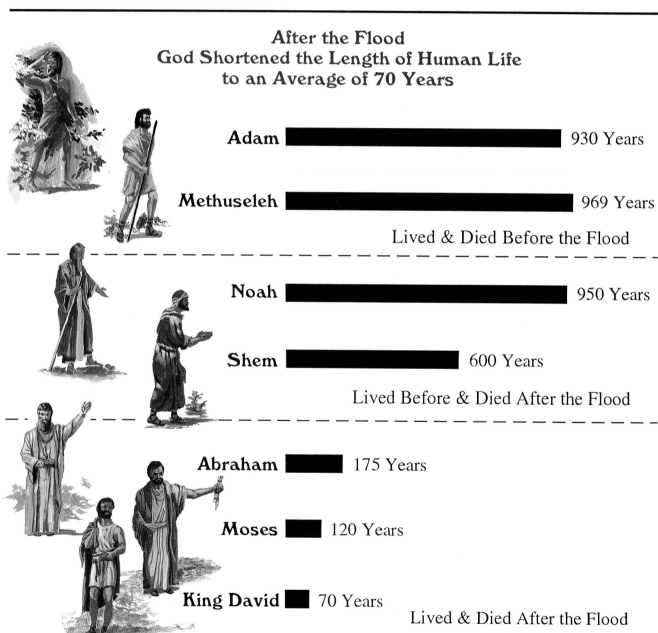

After the Flood
God Shortened the Length of Human Life
to an Average of 70 Years

Adam	930 Years
Methuseleh	969 Years

Lived & Died Before the Flood

Noah	950 Years
Shem	600 Years

Lived Before & Died After the Flood

Abraham	175 Years
Moses	120 Years
King David	70 Years

Lived & Died After the Flood

Before the Flood, when the world was much different than today, people sometimes lived almost one thousand years! But after the Flood, people's lives were much shorter. Today, few people live to be even 100 years old.

"And God looked upon the earth, and indeed it was corrupt; for all flesh had corrupted their way on the earth. And God said to Noah, 'The end of all flesh has come before Me, for the earth is filled with violence through them; and behold, I will destroy them with the earth.'" Genesis 6:12–13

The Lost World Punished

The Bible says that "the earth was filled with violence" (Genesis 6:13). Even the animals were living in a way that their Creator had not intended. Everything that breathed had been changed by sin. If God had not acted to destroy the earth, then even the few men and women who still obeyed Him would have been lost, and the Savior, who had been promised, could not have been born.

But God does not punish those who trust in Him. Noah and his family loved and trusted God, and God warned them of His plans to destroy the world. He told Noah to build an Ark—a huge boat—big enough to provide safety for his family and every kind of animal that lived on the land. It probably took Noah nearly 120 years to build the Ark (Genesis 6:3). During that time, no one else began to love the Lord (Hebrews 11:7). Noah told the people that

God was going to send a Flood to destroy the world and everything in it, but no one listened. He said that if they believed and obeyed God, then they could find safety on the Ark, but they only made fun of him. The people kept on living the way that they wanted (II Peter 2:5).

The end of that beautiful world came suddenly. Seven days after Noah and his family were safely inside the Ark with the animals, rain began to fall (Genesis 7:10). It was not a gentle rain, but rain and hail so powerful that it destroyed life. The people had never before seen rain. Perhaps they quickly realized that the destruction about which Noah had warned them was beginning. But even if they did, it was too late. God had already closed the Ark to protect the people and animals inside (Genesis 7:16). Outside of the Ark, terrified people and animals would try to seek safety, but their opportunity to be saved was lost.

Chapter 2

The Ark and the Flood

The Bible says it was to be 300 cubits long, 50 cubits wide, and 30 cubits high (Genesis 6:15). It was to be a long narrow ship, something like a modern barge.

Noah's Ark was not a small boat. In fact, it was longer than a football field and taller than a four-story building. The measurements that God gave to Noah were in "cubits"—a Hebrew measurement used at that time—which was the distance from a man's elbow to the tip of his fingers, or about 18 inches (about 0.45 meters).

When the measurements of the Ark in Genesis 6:15 are changed to feet, we discover the Ark was about 450 feet long (135 meters), 75 feet wide (23 meters), and 45 feet tall (13 meters). Compare the Ark's size with the size of the modern truck shown in the picture, and imagine now many truckloads of animals and other supplies could be loaded into the Ark!

Some people think that the Ark was too small to carry all of the pairs of animals on board, but most of these people have not taken the time to look at just how big the Ark really was. Nor have they considered how many animals were to be taken on board. It is easy to see that there was room for everything, and simple math shows us there was even extra space left over.

Many story books show pictures of the Ark as some kind of houseboat with a few of the animals on board sticking their heads out the top, but this is certainly not right. The Bible describes Noah's Ark as HUGE! The Ark's "tonnage"—or the amount of weight it could carry—was nearly *forty million pounds (fifteen million kilograms)*! It probably looked much more like a giant cargo ship or enclosed barge, all sealed up tight for protection against the terrible storm to come.

Was Noah's Ark a small boat full of happy animals, or was it more like a huge floating warehouse? The Ark on the left is like the kind you see in most stories. The modern truck in the picture (just for comparison) shows the great size of the real Ark, as described in the Bible.

How Could Noah Build Such a Boat?

Noah and his three sons probably had close to 120 years to build the Ark (Genesis 6:3). The people who lived then were very skilled workers who were able to make almost anything they could imagine, but of course for this project, Noah and his sons followed directions from God. Even if they had never built a ship before, they were probably pretty good carpenters after a year or two! There was plenty of time for them to cut down trees, make lumber, and finish construction on the Ark.

God told Noah to make three decks in the Ark, with rooms that could be used for animal stalls and storage (Genesis 6:14, 16). God also told Noah to cover the Ark inside and out with some kind of "pitch" to keep water from leaking into the rooms.

Noah and his sons may have had a special recipe to cook the pitch, much like the tar we use today for roof repair. This same pitch might also have helped keep the Ark from rotting and being destroyed by the weather after it landed on Mt. Ararat.

How Did Noah Get All the Animals?

Noah and his family did not have to gather the animals themselves. The Bible says that God brought all the animals to Noah in time to get on board (Genesis 6:91-20).

Because all kinds of animals lived much closer together before the Flood, they probably did not have to travel far to get to the Ark. (The world looked much different then, with no high mountains to divide the continents). It was much easier for people and animals to get from place to place than it is today.

How Could All the Animals Fit Inside the Ark?

Pairs of each "kind," or basic type of land-dwelling, air-breathing animal, had to be on board the Ark (Genesis 7:22). We don't know how many kinds were alive in Noah's day, but today there are less than 20,000 different types of animals, not counting those animals who live in the sea, or those who don't breath air. Even most insects were probably not on the Ark. They don't "breathe" air and their eggs and larvae would survive on floating logs outside the Ark.

All modern types could, through small changes, have come from about 5,000 kinds or less that God originally created. But no matter how many kinds there were, we know that the Ark was big enough to haul more than 50,000 animals, with room to spare!

Although there were no doubt many daily chores to do during the months of the Flood, most of the animals would require very little care. Many animals (like bears) hibernate when the weather is bad, and almost every creature will lie very quietly and still when trapped during times of great danger.

The great storm would have been very frightening, with great winds howling, thunder and lightning crashing, and waves pounding all day and all night; but the "survival instincts" that God created within the animals would have kept them rather peaceful through the tossing and rolling of the Ark during the horrible storm.

What Did the Animals Eat on the Ark?

God told Noah to take food on the Ark for the animals and his family (Genesis 6:21). Certainly the animals would not be allowed to eat each other, and they would not be fighting during this time of danger, anyway. There was probably food like hay and corn on board, but because many animals were in a hibernation-like state, Noah and his family did not have to feed them very much at all.

What About the Dinosaurs?

All of the various kinds of land dinosaurs were on the Ark with the rest of the animals. After all, God created them on Day Six along with Adam and Eve. When God brought two animals of *every* kind to board the Ark, the dinosaurs must have been included, too! We know that dinosaurs not only lived along with man before the Flood, but also survived the Flood to live afterward with man.

Sometimes we think about dinosaurs as being vicious, mean beasts, but when God created the world, all animals were to live in peace with each other and with man. Originally, dinosaurs and other creatures ate only plants (Genesis 1:29-30). Today, animals that eat only plants are called "herbivores."

It may be that after Adam and Eve sinned, some of the dinosaurs and other animals became meat-eaters (or "carnivores"), but we do not know exactly when or if this actually happened. Some fossil bones of dinosaurs do look like they were "terrible lizards," but there is no way to know for sure how the great creatures behaved toward each other. All we find are bones of dead ones!

God felt that these powerful creatures were quite special. In the book of Job, the Bible describes two great beasts that we would call ''dinosaurs'' today. The people of Job's day (who lived soon after the Flood) called one of the animals ''Behemoth.'' We can read about God's description of the power and majesty of this awesome creature in Job 40:15-24. The other dinosaurs is called ''Leviathan'' and breathes out smoke and fire like a dragon. You can read about this fearsome marine-dwelling creature in Job Chapter 41.

After reading these verses, what kind of dinosaurs do you think Behemoth and Leviathan were? God calls Behemoth ''chief among His works,'' or in other words, ''king of the land animals.'' of Leviathan He says ''No one is so fierce that dare stir him up.''

The description God gave to Job was one of a very large and powerful dinosaur, with bones like iron and a tail as large and long as a tall cedar tree. This creature might have been an *Apatosaurus* or *Brachiosaurus*, an animal that could have weighed up to 33 tons and eaten 2,000 pounds of green plants every day!

Most dinosaurs were not as big as this giant, however, and God did not need to bring fully grown animals into the Ark. Usually reptiles (including dinosaurs) grow bigger and bigger as long as they live, but Noah probably took young, strong dinosaurs on the Ark—ones much smaller than fully grown dinosaurs. (Modern reptiles, even if they grew to be very old, would not be dinosaurs. Dinosaurs had different hip joints and skull types than any modern reptile.)

Outside the Ark

God sent the Flood as a judgment against the evil, wicked, and violent people of the earth. All the people died. All the land animals died. Many, but not all, fish and other ocean creatures died also. All land creatures that had the breath of life in them were wiped from the face of the earth—all except those on the Ark with Noah and his family (Genesis 7:22-23).

Outside the Ark, after Noah and his family got on board and God closed the door, the wicked people probably continued to make fun of Noah and shout insults at him—until it began to rain. They had never seen it rain before—and no one today has seen it rain as hard as it rained during the first 40 days and 40 nights of Noah's Flood.

The Bible says "on that day all the fountains of the great deep were broken up, and the windows of heaven were opened" (Genesis 7:11), meaning that all of the water below the earth and all of the water above the earth rushed to cover the earth.

Have you ever felt an earthquake? There were countless earthquakes during the time of the Flood, stronger than any that happen today. The earth itself began to shake so powerfully that the evil people outside the Ark knew at once that what Noah had said was true—but it was too late!

The ground split open everywhere as trees and buildings collapsed. Geysers of water, lava, and steam shot up from the cracks of the earth as the ''fountains'' were broken up under the ground.

Geologists have found evidence that many large meteors may have fallen through the sky and smashed into the ground during this time, as well. These huge rocks from space broke up the ground, causing earthquakes and destroying everything for miles around.

Huge walls of rushing water pounded the earth and swept away all that was left of great cities. The Ark did not seem to move at first, but as wave after wave rushed over the ground and crashed into its sides, the great Ark rose above the earth. You probably have been in a terrible rain storm before, but have you ever seen a tornado or hurricane? This storm was the greatest hurricane in history!

Can you imagine being in the Ark, tossed back and forth and up and down as huge waves crashed about you? Although they were safe inside, Noah and his family probably held on to each other in fear, as if they were on a non-stop roller coaster ride!

We can be thankful that we have not seen or been in such a terrible storm. Even after the Flood covered the earth, and the world became one great ocean, the volcanic eruptions continued beneath the water. The earth was being destroyed (II Peter 3:6). It would never again look the same as it did before the Flood.

Ronald

How Did the Flood Cover the Mountains?

The Bible says that during the Flood the water covered even the highest mountain. The water was high enough for the Ark to float right over the top of it (Genesis 7:19–20). The mountains we see today are higher than those that God made when He created the earth. We know this because most of today's mountains are made of many, many layers of mud, now turned to rock, stacked on top of each other by the waters of the Flood.

These rock layers were originally mud. They formed under water as all of the dirt and rocks settled out flat beneath the Flood ocean. Today we can see the layers packed together with billions and billions of fossils of creatures which died during the Flood. The bodies of dead plants and animals were buried in these mud layers, which later dried and became rock.

When these layers (also called "strata") were still soft mud, they could be bent like clay and pushed upward into huge mountains by earth movements during Noah's Flood. Many of the other tall mountains we see now are volcanoes which erupted and grew taller during the Flood and continued to grow after the Flood was over. So we can see that today's mountains were made by the Flood, and were not as high during the Flood as they are now. There is plenty of water on earth to cover those lower mountains before the Flood.

Where Did All the Water Go?

When God decided to end the Flood, He caused the deep ocean floors to form, perhaps by separating the continents. As the waters rushed off, the earth's new surface took shape. Huge canyons, like Grand Canyon, were carved out of the soft earth by the water as it flowed off the land into the new ocean basins.

If the earth's surface were completely smooth, with no high mountains and no deep oceans, the water would be nearly two miles deep! The earth has plenty of water for the Flood. Today the water is in the deep oceans.

Lloyd R. Hight

*Grand Canyon—carved out
by retreating Flood waters.*

The World After the Flood

Toward the end of the Flood, God caused the land to appear. Mountains were suddenly raised up out of the water, as large basins—which are now today's oceans—were made to hold the flood waters.

When you visit or look at pictures of the Grand Canyon, you can see layers upon layers of rocks that were once mud. These rock layers were laid down during Noah's Flood. The deep canyon was cut as the Flood waters raced off the land while the layers were still relatively soft, just as mud or sand can be easily eroded.

In parts of the world, whole forests were ripped out of the ground by the Flood waters. Parts of them were later buried to form large beds of coal, while other organisms were buried in such a way that they turned into oil and gas. These "fossil fuels" are the energy that we use today. The floating logs and plants which didn't get buried under the ground landed on top of the ground as the waters drained away. Insect

eggs on the logs hatched, and seeds and sprigs began to sprout.

When the Ark settled on the mountain, Noah first sent out a raven to see if life outside the Ark was possible. It probably found floating bodies of animals to eat and didn't come back. Noah later sent out a dove, and still later another dove. When it returned, it had a small olive twig in its beak. Later, the dove was able to find a home outside the Ark, and Noah knew that it was safe to leave (Genesis 8:6–13).

We can only imagine what it was like in those days. At first, few things were growing and life was hard for Noah's family and the animals. But it was not long before fast-growing grasses and even flowers sprouted from the moist soil. Shrubs and trees scattered over the earth. Eventually, these plants provided food and homes for the different kinds of animals leaving the Ark.

What About the People?

When Noah, his family, and the animals left the Ark, Noah and offered a sacrifice to God in

Babylon
Babylonian "gods" (idols) told a man to build a boat and fill it with his family, property, cattle, wild beasts, and food. Life on earth was to be destroyed by a great flood. After rain lasting only six days, this Babylonian "Noah" sent out a dove, a swallow, and a raven. When he left the boat, he sacrificed an animal, and the gods were so pleased that they made the man and his wife gods, also.

Greece
In an ancient Greek story a man made a box into which he put all the things necessary for life. When he and his wife shut themselves in the box, the Greek god Zeus caused a great rain to fall. Everyone died except those who climbed to the tops of very high mountains. For nine days and nights the man was tossed on the sea. Finally the box landed and he and his wife left the box.

India
An early story from India tells of a fish that warned a man called Manu about a flood that would kill everything. Like the true story, Manu was told to build a boat, but Manu alone survived the flood.

thankfulness for His protection. Then God spoke to Noah again, and told him that his sons, their children, and their children's children were to fill the whole earth. But after some time, the descendants of Noah's sons had traveled only a few hundred miles from where the Ark had landed. At this time, all people had the same language. It was easy for them to work together and share the same ideas. They decided to disobey God by not spreading across the earth as He had told them to do.

But this disobedience was not the only thing. Ruled by a strong leader named Nimrod, these people built many great cities and decided to build a great tower that would reach high into the heavens (Genesis 11:4). Nimrod led the people to worship the stars, in direct disobedience to God's command to worship Him. Today many people still worship the stars, even though God says it is sin.

God could see that these people were following the same path of disobedience as the people before the Flood, and that nothing they could imagine would be impossible for them to do (Genesis 11:6). But there was a way to stop them from finishing the tower. God gave each family a new language, different from what they had known before. When this happened, the people could not understand each other or work together, so they quit building the high tower. This unfinished structure was named the "Tower of Babel," meaning "Tower of Confusion." The families and groups who spoke the same language left and began journeys to far parts of the earth (Genesis 11:7–9). Some groups soon started mighty nations in Egypt, China, near Israel, and elsewhere. Others lived in caves and jungles with very primitive cultures. God had forced them to fill the new earth, even though they had tried to disobey.

Wherever people went, they would tell their children the story of Noah and the Great Flood. As time went on, some story-tellers would add to or change the true story. Only God's Word, the Bible, still has the true story. Hundreds of such Flood stories, told by people at different times and in different parts of the world, have been collected. Here are a few that show how the true Biblical story has been changed.

NORTH AMERICA

SOUTH AMERICA

THE PACIFIC

North America
In North America, the Lenni Lenape Indians told of a time when a powerful snake made all people wicked. The snake caused water to destroy everything. But on an island was a man named Manabozho, the grandfather of all men. He was saved by riding on the back of a great turtle, not in the Ark as in the true story.

South America
From Peru a story comes about a shepherd and his family. They noticed one day that their llamas were sad, so they studied to find out why. The stars told about a great flood which was coming. The shepherd and his family climbed a high mountain, and as the water rose higher and higher, the top of the mountain began to float so that they were saved.

The Pacific
Even the islands of the Pacific have flood stories. One of these explains how a fisherman got his fishing hook caught in the hair of the ocean god. The god awoke and decided that people were evil and should be destroyed. The fisherman begged for forgiveness, so the god told him to go to an island where he would be safe from the flood he would send.

Chapter 3

The Ark and the Mountain

The Bible doesn't say what happened to the Ark after its landing on Mt. Ararat. Noah and his sons could have taken the Ark apart to build houses and shelters, or, the Ark could have just turned into dust after many years.

But, there are many reasons to believe it is still there. Since the time of the Flood, people all over the world have written or told stories about the Ark. There are many eyewitnesses who say they have seen the Ark while climbing on Mt. Ararat. Others say that they knew people who had seen the Ark. And in recent years, many people claim to have seen the Ark from airplanes.

How Could the Ark Be Preserved?

Today, the top of Mt. Ararat is covered with a glacier—a large area of snow and ice that never completely melts. It is possible that the Ark is in the glacier and can be seen only during the hottest summers, when much of the ice and snow melt away for a few weeks. Naturally, if the Ark is in a glacier, it would be frozen and could not rot. The Bible tells us that Noah put "pitch" all over the Ark, both inside and out. This covering of pitch would also help keep the Ark from rotting.

The Bible says "the Ark rested on the mountains of Ararat" (Genesis 8:4), or the region around the ancient country of "Urartu." Over the years, hundreds of people have claimed to see Noah's Ark high on this mountain, which today is called Mt. Ararat. Most of them say that it is in or near the rocky canyon in this picture called the Ahora Gorge, up near the snow line.

Here is another idea to think about. Mt. Ararat is a volcano. It has erupted many times since the Flood. Sometimes red-hot rock, called lava, flowed out of the volcano. As the lava slowly moved along, it would have burned everything that it touched, including the Ark!

However, when a volcano erupts, it does not always throw out lava. Many times, the volcano blows out great amounts of tiny pieces of dust, which would cover everything in sight. This dust is called volcanic ash. The dust is hot, but not hot enough to burn everything.

If the Ark were covered by a layer of volcanic ash, it would have been protected from any burning lava which came later. After a long time the wood could even have turned to stone, or become petrified. Have you ever seen petrified wood? The best way for wood to turn to stone is for it to be covered by volcanic ash. Many of the people who say they have seen the Ark say it is as hard as stone.

These are two possible ways that the Ark might have been preserved all of these years. The Bible does not teach that the Ark would last, but many people have said that they have seen it. Perhaps some day soon someone will discover the Ark and solve the mystery!

Have People Really Seen Noah's Ark?

What an adventure it would be to explore the Ark! Think about climbing over the roof deck and looking into the windows along the top. Maybe you could get inside the Ark through one of these. Inside you might be able to explore the stalls where the animals were kept and wonder what kind of animals each had held. As you explore you might even find the rooms where Noah and his family stayed while the Flood waters raged against the Ark. Without a doubt, finding Noah's Ark would be one of the major discoveries of our lifetime.

According to the people who live around Mt. Ararat today, 100 years ago people visited the Ark many times. Parents often took their children to see the Ark and explained the story of Noah and the Flood. Many other explorers, airplane pilots, travelers, and shepherds also claim to have seen the Ark. I have heard of and read many such stories and have talked to some of the people. Almost always their stories are very similar. Here are a few stories that are among the most important.

Eyewitness Stories

Around 1905, a shepherd boy named Jacob saw the Ark while trying to find his lost goats. Pictures that he drew show a box-like Ark sticking out of the ice. His drawings show the Ark resting on the edge of a steep drop-off (Sketch A).

In 1908, and again in 1910, another shepherd boy, Georgie, climbed the mountain with his uncle to see the Ark. He even walked on top of the Ark and looked inside the windows. They had to pile up rocks next to the Ark to get on top. Georgie said the Ark was as hard as rock and was covered with boulders and snow in some places (Sketch B).

Often, great mystery surrounds stories about the Ark and the people who have seen it. In 1916 and 1917, soldiers and scientists from

Sketch A

Russia climbed the mountain to see the Ark. They took photographs and drew maps of the Ark. They even went inside and saw stalls where the animals had been. While they were on the mountain, war started in their country, and when they returned home, the pictures were lost. Several of the scientists and soldiers traveled to other countries and were able to tell their stories, but they didn't have the photographs or maps as proof. Then, just a few years ago, we met an old Russian man. He had photographs of the Ark, which he said were taken by the earlier explorers. He showed them to a man who sketched what was in the photographs, but now the mysterious Russian has died and the photographs have disappeared. Nobody knows where these pictures are, but they showed something similar to Sketch C.

Notice how similar all of these drawings are. They show a long, box-like boat with a long window along the top. In all of the drawings, the Ark looks different from any regular boats that the eyewitnesses would have seen or that we could see today. They say it looked more like a barge than a boat. They talk about the row of windows running along the top. All of the witnesses say that only part of the Ark can usually be seen, with the rest of it still covered by rock, ice, and snow. Most of them say it sits on a ledge, with a cliff rising on one side and a steep drop-off on the other. They say it is difficult to get to, but not impossible if you know how to get there.

Sketch B

Sketch C

27

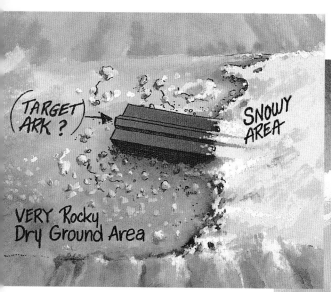

(TARGET ARK ?)

SNOWY AREA

VERY Rocky Dry Ground Area

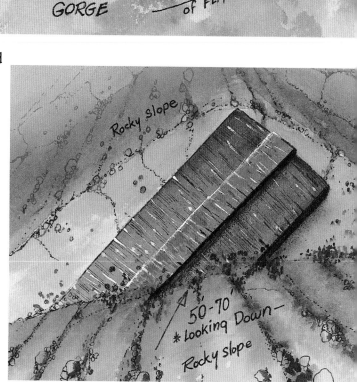

SNOW

ROCK CLIFF

LEDGE

AHORA GORGE

Direction of Flight

Recent Sightings

Many people still living today say that they have seen Noah's Ark from airplanes (Sketch D). Other have climbed to it. Many of them have drawn what they remembered, and all of the drawings look very much the same. I have talked to several of these people, and I believe that they are telling the truth.

Mr. Albert Shappell saw the Ark from a Navy airplane in 1974. He took pictures of the Ark, but was not allowed to keep them. He drew what he remembered (Sketch E). Also in 1974, Mr. Ed Behling saw the Ark. He was taken up to it by an old shepherd who lived on the mountain. He didn't take any pictures, but he recalls that the Ark was sticking out of the mountain, not out of the ice. He was not able to get all of the way down to it without ropes to help him, so he wasn't able to explore the Ark up close (Sketch F).

Usually, people remember details a little differently. As you can see, these drawings are all slightly different. Still, all of them are obviously describing the same thing, and all of the drawings agree with how the Bible describes the Ark (see Chapter 2).

The trouble with these stories is that none of the people have been able to tell exactly where

Rocky slope

50-70' * Looking Down—

Rocky slope

they saw the Ark. Mt. Ararat is a huge and dangerous mountain. Even from the eyewitness accounts, we cannot be sure where to look.

SIDE VIEW OF VESSEL

Sketch G

One friend of Mr. Green remembered two photographs of the Ark. He drew them both in Sketch G. The other friend remembered another photograph, his drawing is Sketch H.

Sketch H

Explorers began looking for the Ark over 50 years ago, but they had only a few hints of where to look. They couldn't actually find anyone who said they had seen it or had even seen good pictures of it. They didn't have all the sketches you saw on pages 27 and 28, so their searches didn't do much good.

One of the first really good clues came from a man whose friend, George Green, had seen the Ark from an airplane in 1953. Mr. Green had taken several good pictures of the Ark and had shown them to lots of people. He wanted to go back and study the Ark.

Unfortunately, Mr. Green died before he could go back to Mt. Ararat, and no one has been able to find his pictures ever since. But his friend remembered what the pictures showed, and drew the sketches one from the side, and one looking at the end of the Ark. They are shown in sketch G.

Later, another friend drew another sketch from his memory of a different view, sketch H. Their drawings are a little different, but still showing the same features seen in all the other sketches.

29

An artist painted this after hearing me give a talk on the search for Noah's Ark. I had shown many slides of the mountain, and the different eyewitness sketches. He drew this picture to include all the different details of all the eyewitnesses.

"Spying" on Noah's Ark

You probably know what a spy does. A spy secretly observes things in other countries. Our government also has spy satellites in outer space, and airplanes which fly high above the ground, taking pictures of things on the ground.

Many people say they have seen secret spy pictures of Noah's Ark taken from satellites or airplanes. One man drew this sketch (I) after seeing some pictures taken from a spy airplane.

Sketch I

The Unidentified Object

Look at the picture on the next page. The object that looks like Noah's Ark was not seen when the picture was taken. We have never been able to find the object again. We don't know what it is, but the object certainly looks like Noah's Ark! Several explorers think that this is a photograph of the Ark, but to examine it we must first find it again. We call it the "Unidentified Object."

Notice that it is in a rocky area with cliffs and ledges. The "Unidentified Object" seems to be on one of the ledges, and sticking back into the cliff. It is very difficult to figure out exactly where this object is, but one of our main goals is to locate and identify this object. It may be a rock—or it may be the Ark!

The photo of the
"Unidentified Object"
was taken by an
expedition in the 1960's.
No one is sure who took
the picture or exactly
where it is located. We
need to rediscover and
"identify" the
"Unidentified Object."

31

Davis Canyon

Recently, I met a man named Mr. Ed Davis. Years ago, when he was a soldier in the U.S. Army, some of the local people near Mt. Ararat became his friends. They took him up on the mountain and showed him the Ark. Much later an artist named Elfred Lee listened to his story and carefully drew this picture. Mr. Davis explained each detail as he remembered it, even the place where he says he saw the Ark—a canyon we now call the Davis Canyon.

Of course, we must be careful before we draw too many conclusions about where the Ark will be found. It is possible for a rock or piece of ice to be in a box-like shape. If we are not careful, we could make a mistake and think that we are seeing the Ark when we are not. Just climbing the mountain is very dangerous and difficult, so it's nice to know where to look.

In recent years, we have been able to use pictures taken by satellites in outer space to help us search for Noah's Ark. So far we haven't seen anything that we know is the Ark, but several interesting shapes can be seen to which we want to climb and study.

The Mystery Object

What do you see in this picture? A friend of mine took the photo shown on the next page by holding his camera out over the edge of a cliff. It was too dangerous for him to reach the edge and look over, but he was able to take several pictures of the hidden canyon below. When the film was developed and the pictures examined, a strange object that looks like Noah's Ark could be seen, just as these two enlargements of the photo in the upper left show. But because he didn't actually see the object himself, we don't know for certain what it really is. In fact, the more we study the picture, the less we believe it to be the Ark—but we certainly plan to go back and take a closer look!

Mr. Ed Davis' description of the Ark, drawn by Elfred Lee. We are not exactly sure where this area is.

The Mystery Object

These three illustration are all taken from the same photo—The Mystery Photo—taken of the Mystery Object. In the upper left it shows the object as actually seen in the photo. Remember, this is probably *not* Noah's Ark. But if it isn't—what could it be?

Chapter 4

Adventure On Ararat

Many people have gone to Mt. Ararat to try to find Noah's Ark. I have been there more than ten times.

The first time that I climbed Mt. Ararat, I was looking for the strange "unidentified object" in the picture on page 31. Because the glacier moves down the mountain, and rocks of all sizes continually shift and move downhill, I did not know exactly where to look. The mountain changes a little each day of the year.

There are few mountains as dangerous to climb as Mt. Ararat. Things happened during each of my climbs to make me believe that Satan was trying to keep us from finding the Ark. Satan knows that if Noah's Ark is found, many people's eyes will be opened and they will believe the Bible.

Danger!

Many times while climbing we were nearly hit by falling rocks. Some of these rocks were boulders bigger than a car. At times, hundreds of rocks would start rolling down the mountain as fast as a runaway truck. They would easily crush anyone they hit. Even the smaller rocks could kill. Some climbers have been seriously injured, and others even killed on Mt. Ararat. We are thankful that God has protected us and that none of the people climbing with me have ever been hit by these rock slides.

The ice and snow are also very dangerous. Sometimes deep caves are hidden beneath a thin snow cover, and if a climber fell into one, he might never get out. The ice also has cracks in it which are big enough for a man to fall into. Many climbers have fallen into these cracks; some have suffered broken bones, and other have died. Often snow and ice break loose from the top of the mountain and slide down the mountain slope, covering everything, including climbers. At times we have been caught in violent storms that buried our tents. During these storms, we could not get out and had to

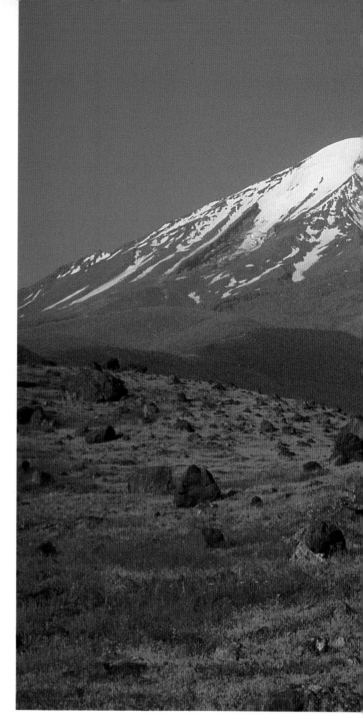

stay in our sleeping bags with all our coats and clothing on to keep from freezing.

But these are not all of the dangers. Wild animals also live on Mt. Ararat. The worst are the wild wolf-like dogs. These dogs are bigger than German Shepherds, but much meaner (and really ugly)! Many of the people living near the mountain keep these mean, ugly dogs and train them to attack and even kill strangers. Several times we have been attacked. We have been thankful that we could keep them away with our sharp ice axes and by throwing rocks at them.

Here the author is searching an area with binoculars before climbing through the crevasses.

35

Struck by Lightning

The most difficult and most frightening adventure during our first search for the Ark happened as two friends and I were climbing near the top of the mountain. Many times on the mountain we have had to climb in snow storms, but this day there was a lightning storm! We were so high that we were actually up in the clouds. Suddenly, thunder hammered around us so loudly it almost made us go deaf. Rocks and boulders close by began making a humming noise. Electricity in the air made the hair on our heads, faces, and arms stand straight out. Then, with a sudden blinding flash, all three of us were hit by lightning.

The lightning hit my body like a truck. The power of the lightning bolt threw me about 100 feet down the mountain. As I fell, everything was black—I couldn't see and I didn't know what was happening. After rolling, bumping, and slamming into many big rocks, I finally stopped, and at the same time my eyes began to clear. I could see again.

For a few minutes I just lay in the snow, hurting all over. But when I tried to get up, I couldn't! The lightning had damaged all of the muscles in my legs and they wouldn't move. No longer were my legs strong; now they were soft, like jelly. I called out to my two friends for help, but no one answered. Soon I saw that they also had been hit by lightning and were just as hurt as I was.

When the lightning hit us, we had already been climbing for two days and we were far away from our friends in the base camp lower on the mountain. Even if they came to look for us, there was no hospital nearby. All three of us thought we were going to die.

Preparing to Die

At that moment, I found that I wasn't afraid to die. Because I am a Christian, I knew that I would go to be with Jesus in Heaven if I died. Memories of when I was a child began flooding into my mind. As I lay paralyzed in the cold snow, I remembered my father telling me stories about Jesus when I was 5 or 6 years old . One night, while sitting on his lap, I asked Jesus to come into my life. As a child, I knew that I had been mean to my brothers and sisters, disobeyed my parents, told lies, and did other things that God calls sin. My father told me how Jesus Christ had come to die on the cross to save me from my sins. He told me how God would forgive my sins and come to live within me and help me to do the things that please Him. That night, I had asked God to forgive me for my sins and thanked Him for sending Jesus to be my Savior. From that time on I knew that I was a Christian, one of God's special children. And so, while I didn't want to die, I wasn't afraid.

But God had other plans for me and didn't let me die that day on Mt. Ararat. I began to recall Bible verses that I had memorized as a child—verses that said God can make a sick person well. I realized that God wanted me well again. He could make my legs strong again, just as easily as He made the lame man walk in the Bible.

And God did heal me as I prayed to Him. Soon I was walking around, taking care of my two friends, and before long, God made their bodies strong again, too.

The storm still swirled all around us, with lightning striking everywhere, but we continued up the mountain to search for Noah's Ark. We praised God that He had worked a miracle that day to make us well.

Back to Ararat!

Since then, we have been back to Turkey and Mt. Ararat many times to look for the Ark. Other explorers, most of whom are friends of mine, have also tried to find the Ark. Many interesting things have been discovered, including some more mysterious photographs, but as of yet, the Ark has not been found.

Some of these searches have been made from airplanes or helicopters. Others have used scientific equipment to help determine if something is buried in the snow and ice. Sometimes we use pictures taken from satellites in outer space. But there are many places on the mountain where the Ark could be hidden.

In the next chapter, I will show you some of the new information discovered by me or some of my friends. I would be thankful if God allowed me to find the Ark, but I know someone else may find it instead. That's OK too. Meanwhile, as you will see, the search is very frustrating.

My son Timmy wants to help me look for the Ark when he grows up, if it has not been found by then. Maybe you would like to climb the mountain and look for the Ark. Now that you know the true story of Noah's Ark and what it looks like, maybe you can start your own expedition!

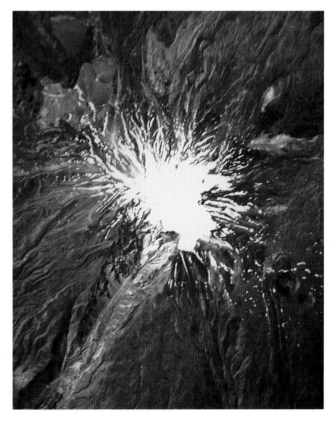

Satellite picture of Mt. Ararat, taken from outer space by LANDSAT.

Chapter 5

The Search Goes On!

Almost every search for the Ark has been on foot, backpacking and camping out. The first time the Turkish government even allowed us to use a helicopter in the search was in 1984. Earlier that year, a friend of mine had noticed something interesting in one of his photographs.

It was in this area that wood was found back in 1955. You can see from the picture that it was not just a log, but a square piece of wood, probably from a building, or maybe Noah's Ark. We wanted to check it out.

Instead of waiting about a week for the helicopter to arrive, my team of explorers climbed to the place in the photograph. We were able to see that the interesting object in the photo was only a deep crack in the ice and rock. We were disappointed, but we hurried back down the mountain to meet the helicopter, intending to search other areas from the air. Our hopes were crushed as the government took back the helicopter and would not allow us to fly at all.

In 1955, a French explorer found long timbers down in a crevasse. He chopped off this piece. Could it be from the Ark?

A glacier is like a frozen waterfall. The wood was found on the left *side of the glacier shown at the top of this page. The interesting crack was on its* right *side.*

The same glacier, as seen from an airplane, is shown on the right.

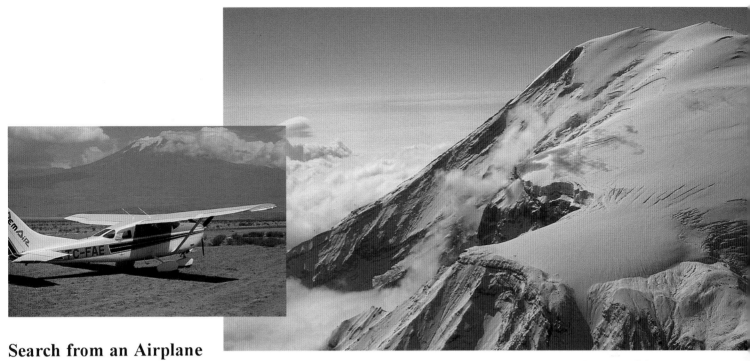

Search from an Airplane

Several times, explorers have been able to use airplanes in the search. Most of the time the planes could not get close enough to the mountain. The winds on any mountain make it very dangerous to fly too close, and the Turkish pilots did not want to crash. But in 1987, we were granted permission to use an airplane, and our pilot was very brave. He had flown on mountains before and knew how to be careful. I wanted to search the canyon (now called the Davis canyon) where we thought Mr. Ed Davis had been when he saw the Ark. No one had since been in this little canyon to check.

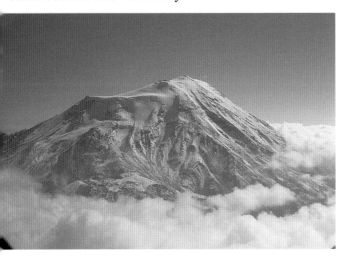

The Davis Canyon lies at the far edge of the cup-shaped canyon. The "Mystery object" is up at the very top of the Ahora Gorge, where the rocky slope meets the glacier.

It is very difficult to get this kind of permission from the government, and very expensive to use an airplane to search. And many times when we do get the permission and pay all the money, we still are not allowed to use the plane to see the things we want.

On this trip, the government said we were allowed to fly as much as we wanted. But the military people near the mountain let us take only one flight on a very cloudy day. The policeman in charge was trying to bully us. He did not even think we would see the mountain that day. But sometimes clouds are only close to the ground; up above the clouds the sky is clear.

That is what happened this day. It was beautiful up above the clouds, but a lot of snow had fallen the night before, covering most of the mountain. The clouds which remained still covered the lower part of the mountain, including the Davis Canyon. We wanted to take more flights when the weather was nicer, but they would not let us.

Searching Davis Canyon

On my first expedition to Mt. Ararat I thought the "Unidentified Object" might be up near the area we now call the Davis Canyon. When I tried to climb up to it, avalanches continually fell around us. It was too dangerous to go that way. Mr. Davis, many years later, told us he went up another way, but that would have been dangerous too.

No one has been allowed to climb into the Davis Canyon since we met Mr. Davis in 1986. But in 1988, two friends of mine did something even better. On separate flights, they were able to fly into that canyon in helicopters.

Remember, Mr. Davis tried his best to tell us where he had seen the Ark, but he had not taken any pictures, and was now too old to go back, himself. It had been over 40 years since he had seen the Ark, and we wondered if he could accurately remember all the details, or maybe we would not be able to figure out exactly where he had been, just from what he could tell us.

The helicopters were powerful enough to fly into the canyon which we think is the Davis Canyon. The mountain is very steep and rugged here, and the explorers could not land and search on foot. But they were able to

The peak of Mt. Ararat is 17,000 feet high. The "Mystery Object" is just below the peak, where the rocks meet the ice cap. We call the snow field near the bottom of the picture, which looks like an upside down valentine heart, the "heart-shaped glacier." The Davis Canyon is just below it.

(Left) Here we can look straight down on the Davis Canyon from a helicopter. Could anything be in here? Very confusing.

(Below) A helicopter picture of the area of the "Mystery Object."

photograph and search thoughout the entire Davis Canyon while leaning out of the helicopter. Unfortunately they didn't see anything that looked at all like the Ark.

Where was Ed Davis when he saw the Ark? Was he somewhere else? Is the Ark really in this canyon and buried under rock? I do not know.

The helicopters were *not* powerful enough to go all the way up to the location of the "Mystery Object." Others have tried to see it from above, but there is usually too much snow to see anything. We still have not been able to check that area as well as we would like.

43

Is the Ark in the Glacier?

Ice and snow cover much of the mountain's top. Some of this ice never melts, even in the hottest summer. Perhaps the Ark is frozen inside this ice (called a glacier), and sticks out only during some years, when more ice melts than is usual.

Some of my friends have tried to search the ice. One group used a special saw to cut a deep trench down into a likely place. Then they used a long drill to go down even further. They worked very hard, but found nothing.

They used scientific equipment to tell them if anything was hidden in the ice. This equipment sends a signal into the ice and measures how the signal "echoes" back to them. In this way, they have found that the Ark is not under the ice near the trench. Others have used the same type of equipment to check in other places. But they have not finished checking all of the huge glacier.

A Careful Study of the Whole Mountain

Over the years the entire mountain has been photographed from the air. These photographs, such as Jim Irwin's picture (above), were able to help us plan our climbs. But they were not very helpful in searching for the Ark

In 1988, another friend of mine was allowed to carefully photograph every place on the mountain from an airplane. This may be the most important study of all.

Using special cameras and film, they took thousands of pictures. A special viewer allows these pictures to be seen in 3-D. They can be studied by a computer, and any interesting objects can be found. They can even see sheep on the mountain and the tents of the shepherds.

Unless the Ark was covered by ice or snow or rock, they should be able to see it. But since they are looking straight down, it might be hard to recognize things on the ground.

Some things have been found in the pictures which now need to be studied up close. Explorers need to look at them, either on foot or from a helicopter.

The Ice Cave

One year we thought the Ark *had* been found. In 1989, some friends of mine had permission to use a helicopter to study the Davis Canyon and the glacier. But they had to park the helicopter in a nearby village.

One morning, as they were flying around the mountain, heading toward the Davis Canyon, they saw something which looked like the Ark. It was a dark hole, or cave, in a glacier which we had never studied. The Turks call this hole "the eye of the bird," because the nearby ice is in the shape of a bird's head, and the hole looks like its eye. We call it the "Ice Cave."

My friends discovered this almost by accident. At first they were sure they had found the Ark. Doesn't it look like all the eyewitness sketches?

They faxed me this sketch from Turkey after their discovery. It looks like the Ark, but the actual Ice Cave doesn't quite look this way.

46

My friend telephoned me from the village that night and said, "John, we have found the Ark!" They even sent me a sketch of what they had seen. I was so excited.

But when they returned to America in two weeks and showed me the video taken from the helicopter, we realized that we needed to go back. Maybe this was the Ark, but we needed to know for sure. The object looked just like all the other sketches. It had a top layer and an opening underneath. The size was about right, too. It even looked petrified. We wanted to get some pieces of it to study with a microscope. Even if it was petrified, we would still be able to see the tree rings.

With God's help we were able to get another helicopter permit and return to the mountain one month later. Even though fall had already come to the mountain, the weather was still good. We flew almost right into the open side of the object.

From a distance, it looked like the Ark. But the closer we got, the more it looked like a rock. As much as I was hoping it was the Ark, I must say I think it is a rock.

To be sure, we needed to get pieces to study. But the government would not allow us to do that. So we do not know absolutely for sure, but I believe it is only a natural feature.

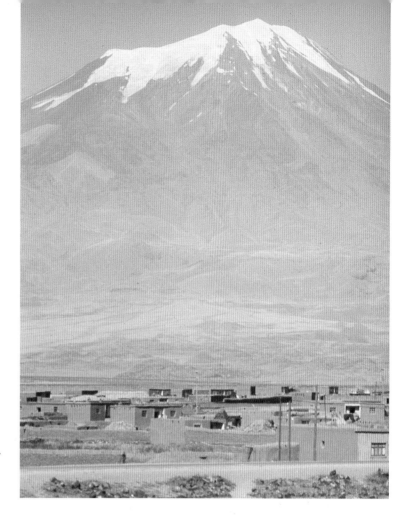

Petrified wood from before the Flood has tree rings, the same as trees do today. The rings were just about all the same, not all different as in today's trees. Some people think trees before the Flood would not have had rings since the weather was pleasant all year long. But there still were seasons (Genesis 1:14), and all trees need to have both times of growth and times of rest to be strong.

"The Eye of the Bird"—high on the slopes of Mt. Ararat is an area that looks like an open bird's beak, made out of glacier ice? The hole in the ice, just about where a bird's eye would be, is the area we studied. You can see this spot even from the village at the base of the mountain.

The Boat-Shaped Mound

About 15 miles away from Mt. Ararat lies a very interesting mound. From an airplane, it looks like it might be a boat, and it is long enough to be the Ark. A few people think it *is* the Ark.

It was formed as the soil on the hillside slid down the hill past a solid rock. This is just like water flowing around a rock in a stream. The movement makes the area look "boat-shaped."

The rock and soil which make up the shape are the same as the rock and soil on nearby hills. There is nothing unusual about this rock except its weird "boat" shape.

Those few people who feel this unusual boat-shaped mound might be Noah's Ark feel that the Ark's material has decayed or petrified.

But they claim to have a lot of evidence. By using a metal detector they say they have found

The "boat-shaped" mound, shown from two directions. You can see Mt. Ararat in the distance.

metal from the Ark's structure inside the mound. They claim to be able to see the "ribs" and "decks" of the ship. They even claim to have found animal remains, like horns and dung. Actually, only a very few people think this is the Ark, and even their ideas are all different.

I have studied this rocky shape for several years. As you can see from the picture above, showing the eroded (rib-like) edge, it consists only of rock covered by soil. It provides good pasture for sheep and goats (horns and dung).

Samples of each rock type have been studied under a microscope. If it was petrified wood it should show rings and tiny wood cells, as does the photomicrograph (microscope picture) of the pre-Flood wood in the upper right.

The photomicrograph on the right is of a rock taken from the mound. This rock is a basalt, or lava rock. Basalt has a lot of metal in it which would be sensed by a metal detector.

The photomicrograph below shows limestone from the mound full of tiny little fossils. This rock and other layers are identical to the layers in the surrounding hills (decks?—No!). This rock was deposited as mud during Noah's Flood and the fossils are remains of pre-Flood sea creatures (like snails).

I wish I could say this object was the Ark, but it's not. It's just a rock!

A photomicrograph of petrified wood, from before the Flood, found in Australia.

Other Places to Check

It may sound like we have been able to search all the mountain now, but we have never been able to check out other areas of interest. Every time we go, we cannot even use our permits and planes the way we need to.

Even worse, thieves and outlaws live on the mountain. In the last few years, especially since the war with Iraq, terrorists have lived on the mountain who capture or kill climbers. Looking for the Ark is not always fun, but it is an adventure.

Chapter 6

Archaeological Discoveries

Expeditions to Mt. Ararat usually have to wait for weeks before they can begin to search. It takes a long time to get permission to climb or fly over the mountain. We like to use this time wisely. There are many other, very interesting, places and things to discover around Mt. Ararat. These ancient discoveries tell us more about the history of the area.

Where would Noah have lived after he came down the mountain once the Flood was over?

We do not know for sure, but probably he would have lived nearby for several years. At least some of his children or grandchildren would have probably lived nearby. We should find some ancient remains of these people.

Archaeology (ar-key-ol-ogy) is the study of ancient remains. Many times, people leave temples, tombs, houses, carvings or other things behind when they leave or die. Today we can study these remains. My friends and I have discovered many such places. Some are only a few hundred years old, others are ancient.

As you have read, we have not found the Ark. But all of the evidence we have found makes us want to keep on looking.

Do you see those caves in the cliff above? Those caves are actually dug out by someone. Through a telescope we can see doors and stairs that these people used. I do not know how old these are, but I do not think they are as old as Biblical times.

They are also similar to underground cities dug in other places in Turkey by Christians (such as Urgup on page 50). Many times people would try to kill all the Christians they could find. In order to escape their enemies, Christians lived underground. Maybe these cliff dwellings above were dug for safety.

Isak Pasha

This beautiful castle on the right was destroyed by a war not long ago. In these pictures, you can still see many of the details carved into the pink rock. The owner was so proud of his castle that he did not want anyone else to have such a beautiful castle, so he cut off the hands of the one who had built it for him. Isn't it awful what a person can do if he does not know God?

Hand-Carved Cave

Near the castle, we studied an ancient cave. It was carved into the hard rock by someone, long, long ago.

From my pictures, archaeologists can tell that the cave may be as old as Noah. Remember, Noah lived for over 300 years after the Flood. This cave may be a tomb. Someone very important may have been buried in there.

We know the tomb is ancient because of the pictures carved into the rock around the opening. Can you see them? There are two people, probably priests, one on each side. The carving of an animal, maybe a sheep or goat, is above the opening.

This appears to be a picture of a sacrifice, like the Bible talks about in the Old Testament. Remember, Noah made a sacrifice to God after he left the Ark.

Inside, the cave is empty. But a staircase goes down into a lower level. We could not go down there without digging because the ceiling has fallen in. Maybe this is where the tomb would be. I wish someone would find out.

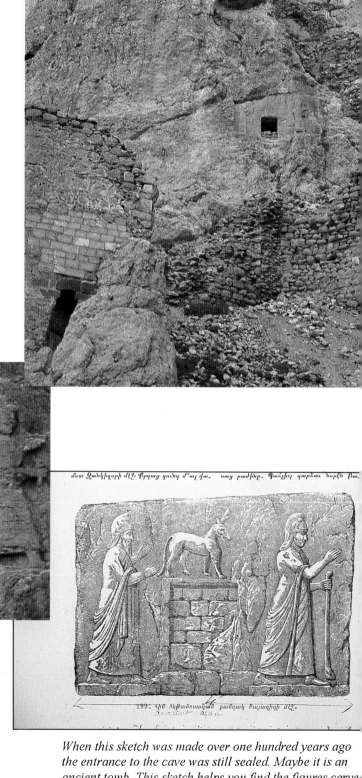

When this sketch was made over one hundred years ago the entrance to the cave was still sealed. Maybe it is an ancient tomb. This sketch helps you find the figures carved into the rock around the opening shown in the picture.

The Black Castle

On the other side of the mountain, we made some very interesting discoveries. In fact, this area is right below where we think the Ark might be.

At the top of a hill halfway up the mountain we found a stone structure. It is open on one side with steps going up into it, flat on one side and round on the other two. The shepherds who live on the mountain now call it "The Black Castle," but they do not know who built it or how old it is. I think it might be an altar. I wonder if it might be the altar which Noah built after the Flood.

The structure seems to have been the main feature of an area with many objects of interest. Evidently for centuries people lived around here and used the "alter" as a center of their attention. Perhaps the descendants of Noah worshipped at the "alter" he built, to aid them in remembering the Lord.

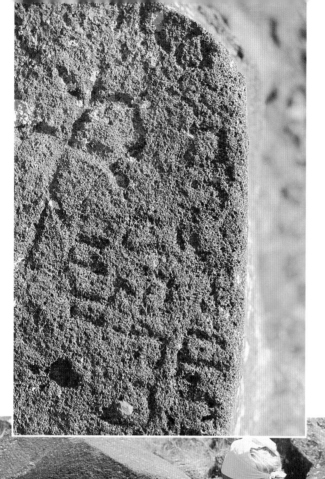

The reason I think it might be so old is that we found many other things there which are very, very old. We found some ancient writing which can not be completely understood, but speaks of religious things. I am told by language scientists that it may be the most ancient writing ever discovered.

Below the altar, we found a rock with eight crosses on it. Almost every nation used crosses in their worship, even long before Jesus died on the cross. These crosses are the type used long, long ago, soon after the Flood. Eight crosses, eight people on the ark. Hmmmm... I wonder.

Below the rock is a cave which contains many pieces of pottery and other objects (as well as snakes). One must be very careful when entering.

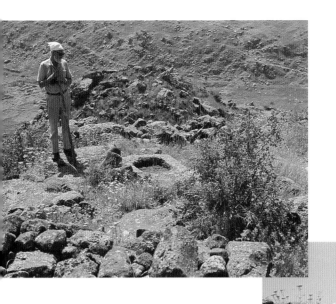

Nearby, we discovered many other things. No one has really studied these since we discovered them. I wish someone would. What secrets do you think we could learn about these ancient people?

On the left you see an unusual rectangular depression of unknown use. Perhaps it was used as a statue base.

At the foot of the "Black Castle" hill are the ruins of a large structure. The shepherds call it "The House of Shem," Noah's son. I don't think it's that old, but it does have some ancient inscriptions, as you see on the left.

What Can We Learn?

One thing we do know for sure. We know these discoveries are not from people who lived *before* the Flood. The Bible says the Flood destroyed the entire world. Everything on the earth was changed. No cities or homes or caves or anything else remain from before the Flood.

Fossils are found near Ararat in layers of rock which were laid down as mud during the Flood. All of these fossils are ocean creatures, like clams and fish, that lived before the Flood. They were buried in the mud and became fossilized, as the bodies of the creatures decayed and were replaced by minerals.

Land animals and even people were also destroyed by the Flood, but their bodies floated around until they were eaten or came apart. They did not sink to the bottom and become fossils. Archaeology studies things which belonged to people *after* the Flood. They were built or buried by people who came from Noah and his family.

These discoveries are surely interesting. From them we can learn many things about the people who lived soon after the Flood, maybe even Noah himself.

Wouldn't it be wonderful if we could find the Ark, also? I am sure that then we could learn even more about the people who lived before the Flood, too.

The twin peaks of Greater and Lesser Mount Ararat

Chapter 7

Will God Send Another Flood?

The Bible doesn't say that the Ark will be found. If someone does find it, pictures of the Ark will be in all the newspapers and on TV for everyone to see. But people do not need to see Noah's Ark to find Jesus and ask Him to save them from their sins. God has made Himself known to everyone through the Bible and also the things that He has made (Romans 1:20). The earth, outer space, the oceans, and all living things remind us that God is the One who made us—He is the One who is our King. And since God is King we need to obey Him. But people today can be just as sinful as the people in Noah's day. Because God hates sin and is a perfect judge, He promises to punish sin just as He did with the people from before the Flood.

Will God send another Flood? No! God promised that He would never send another flood to cover the earth like the great Flood of Noah's day. But God still promises that those who disobey will be punished. The Bible teaches that "the wages (or penalty) of sin is death" (Romans 6:23). This kind of death is not only the death of our bodies. The Bible tells us of a place called Hell. Many times Jesus warned us that anyone who does not ask God to forgive his sins must go to Hell after his body dies. It is a terrible, hurting place away from friends, family and, most of all, away from Jesus, the One who made us and loved us enough to die for our disobedience.

The Good News!

But here is the good news! God will not punish those who have asked Him to be their Savior. We can enjoy Heaven with Him forever. Remember that when God punished the sinful people by sending the Flood, He gave them an opportunity to be saved. But only Noah and his family believed God and only they were saved.

In a very special way, Jesus Christ is like an Ark to us. The Bible says "the gift of God is eternal life through Christ Jesus our Lord"

(Romans 6:23). We can live forever with God because "Christ died for our sins" (1 Corinthians 15:3). Jesus Christ is God's Son. He never sinned, but chose to be punished for our sins instead of us.

Because He died on the cross, we do not have to be punished for our sins. Just as Noah and his family were safe on the Ark, we can be safe with Jesus Christ as our Savior. "For God so loved the

"But as the days of Noah were, so also will the coming of the Son of Man be. For as in the days before the flood, they were eating and drinking, marrying and giving in marriage, until the day that Noah entered the ark, and did not know until the flood came and took them all away, so also will the coming of the Son of Man be."
Matthew 24:37–39

world that He gave His only begotten Son, that whoever believes in Him should not perish, but have everlasting life" (John 3:16).

The Bible promises that Jesus, our Creator, will come back and rule the earth some day. Again, all the violent and evil people who hate God will die. Jesus will then make the earth even better than it was before Adam and Eve disobeyed. Once again the earth will be a wonderful place. The people

who have asked Jesus to save them from the punishment for their sins will live together in peace. The Bible describes that new earth like this, "And I saw a new heaven and a new earth...and God shall wipe away all tears from their eyes; and there shall be no more death, neither sorrow, nor crying, neither shall there be any more pain: for the former things are passed away (Revelation 21:1,4).

And God said: "This is the sign of the covenant which I make between Me and you, and every living creature that is with you, for perpetual generations: I set My rainbow in the cloud, and it shall be for the sign of the covenant between Me and the earth. It shall be, when I bring a cloud; and I will remember My covenant which is between Me and You and every living creature of all flesh; the waters shall never again become a flood to destroy all flesh. The rainbow shall be in the cloud, and I will look on it to remember the everlasting covenant between God and every living creature of all flesh that is on the earth."

Genesis 9:12-16 (NKJ)

A Special Word

The Bible teaches us that we can pray to God and ask Him to forgive us for our sins and bring us into His loving family.

Prayer is simply talking to God. He hears you when you pray out loud or even when you think to yourself. He loves you very much. If you are ready to become one of His children, then here is a prayer that you can pray:

"Lord Jesus, I know that I am a sinner. I do many things that make you unhappy. Sometimes I disobey your rules, I am selfish and I want my own way. Dear God, I am sorry for these sins and I want to please you. I ask you to forgive me for my sins. I am thankful that Jesus loved me so much that He let Himself be punished instead of me. Please help me to obey you and live in a way that will please you. And thank you, God, for hearing me and for forgiving my sins. Amen."

day
0

God Shuts the Door
Noah & His Family are Sealed Within the Ark (Gen. 7:16).

day
7

Flood Begins

Waters trapped deep in the ground break open on the land and the rain begins. There were 40 days of hard rain, volcanic eruptions, erosion, earthquakes and more (Gen. 7:12,17). Waters cover the whole earth (Gen. 7:18–20). All land creatures die (Gen. 7:21–22).

day
47

Day 40 of Flood— Intense Rainfall Ends
For 110 more days, the waters covered the earth (Gen. 7:24), as the rain and eruptions continued. Many layers of mud were laid down, full of dead things. These have now turned into rocks and fossils.

Finally, the water begins to go down.

day
157

Ark Lands on the "New" Mountains of Ararat (Gen. 8:4)
For 74 days, Noah and his family wait while the water continues to go down. A great wind (Gen. 8:1) helps to drive the water off the land. The mountains continue to rise and valleys form. The flood waters continue to collect in the new oceans.

7 days — **40 days** — **110 days** — **74 days**

Dedication

This book is dedicated to four very special people—my wife, Dalta, and my three children, Chara, Tim, and Beth, for whom it was primarily written.

Acknowledgments

The author would like to express his deep appreciation to the following people for their assistance and support in helping make this book a reality: Gloria Clanin, Mark Dinsmore, Robert Doolan, Ken Ham, Ron Hight, Jim Irwin, Elfred Lee, Henry Morris, Mary Thomas, Dave Unfred, and Carl Wieland.

day 231

Other Mountains Appear

For 40 more days, all in the Ark wait while plants begin to grow (Gen. 8:7).

day 271

Noah Sends Out a Raven (Gen. 8:7)

After each of four 7-day periods, Noah sends out a dove (Gen. 8:8,10,12). The water level keeps dropping.

day 299

Last Dove Sent Does Not Come Back

Noah waits 22 more days while the earth continues to dry.

day 321

Most of the Water is off the Land

For 57 more days, the land dries until it is dry enough for animal life (Gen 8:14).

day 378

Leaving the Ark

Noah, his family, and all of the animals leave the Ark to make homes on the changed land.

Noah Built Altar (Gen. 8:20)

Rainbow (Gen. 9:14)

— **40 days** — **28 days** — **22 days** — **57 days** —

Illustrations

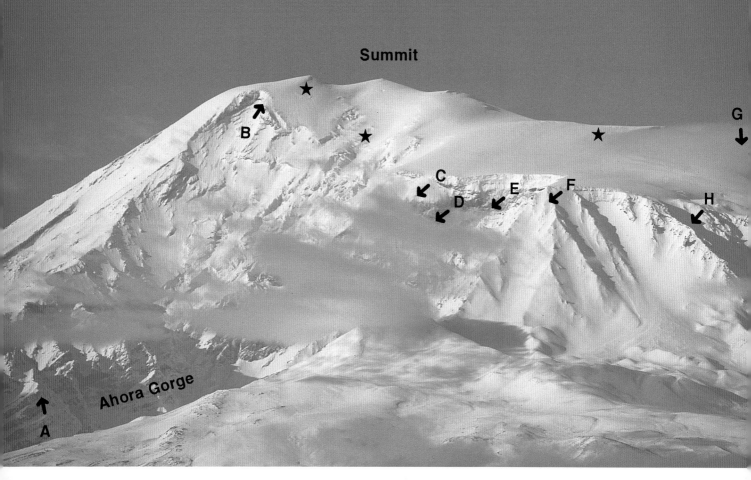

Summit

B

A

Ahora Gorge

C
D
E
F
G
H

Key to Locations on the
North Side of Mt. Ararat

Ahora Gorge — 25, 35, 41
Summit — 43
A. Possible site for the
   "Unidentified Object" – 30
B. "Mystery Object" – 33, 42
C. Heart-shaped glacier – 43
D. Davis Canyon – 32, 41, 42
E. Cup-shaped canyon – 41
F. Struck by lightning – 36
G. Ice Cave – 46
H. Wood found by Frenchman – 40
★ Other areas we want to search

★ A Turkish friend of mine saw this unusual "barn-shaped" object.
We need to check it out!

The Adventure Continues . . . !